HACK o WEEN

(Originally Saved as Document 47)

The Unpublished Works of 2023

Filtering life, law, and society through the lens of
rape survival within a family context

Published By
Self-Publishing Company
Natural Flowism Ltd
Trading as
Natural Flowism Studios

Brain Maturity Age Recommended: 28+

About Cover Art

Is called Telethapy
Part of the retexturizing cotton collection of 2022
a Set of pillows sold at
HOUSE of FLOWISM SHOP
Which is based at
NATURAL FLOWISM STUDIOS
www.naturalflowism.com/house-of-flowism-shop

Telethapy
as
HACK o WEEN
Can also be found
at
www.saatchiart.com/LaviniaDeAyr

Table of Contents

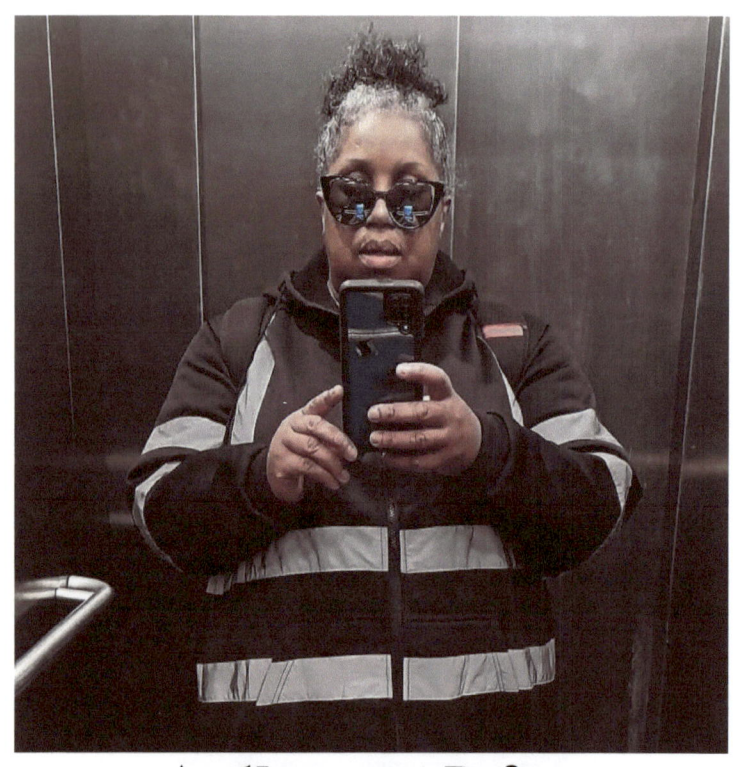

**Author as: Drive
Latter part of 2023
Back in Work
Thank God!
#laviniadeayr**

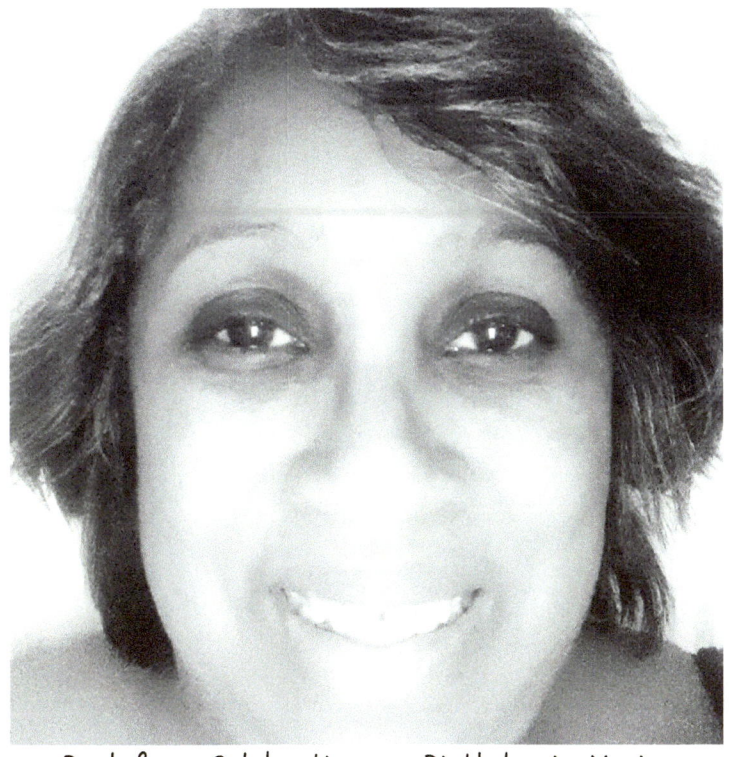

Back from Celebrating my Birthday in Mexico
January 2023
This
Is
Lavinia De Ayr

ABOUT
POETICAL AUTHOR

Lavinia De Ayr got the job as author, main artist, producer, singer, songwriter as an already a self-published poet when she started her own company, and called it,
Natural Flowism LTD

Supply and demand and the need to solve problems have been the root cause of many business formations.

This was also the case when Lavinia, formed her first company, and her second...which in fact are her 3rd & 4th company formations.

Disturbed, and living devastated.
Devastated, and living disturbed.

Whichever way you look at it or describe it, that was the supply and demand that started the poetic author's journey behind the scenes of freedom as a ghost writer of her own book series. Self-healing from experiences such as a sexual molestation from baby through to rape whilst growing up amongst her family.

During her childhood Lavinia begins to pen her own songs, growing up she loved English as a subject at school, which helped her with keeping a day-to-day diary after she was very generously gifted one at aged 15 going on to develop and hone the very powerful healing art of free flow journal writing whilst attending a very brief course at a community college.

With 50+ books under her belt made up of a fusion of her art and poetry from incidents spanning her life a lingering undercurrent of the continuum of childhood sexual abuses morphing into continual targeting possibly better known as the experience of being stalked, all naturally add up to create a catalogue of ongoing experiences mysteries included.

It is not at all hard to recognize how important it is to share individual experiences of abuse endured least of all to raise the incidents themselves, but also to build awareness levels in wider communities.

ABOUT HACK o WEEN SERIES

It is 31st of January 2024
Thanks be to God for this return
and beginning!

Twenty, twenty three was the first
time since 2015 that Lavinia did not
get around to publishing any new
Self-healing works.

A series of setbacks in 2022
practically knocked out publishing
for 2023, making 2023 more of a
year of preparation as she wrestled
with inaction which left her worried
her businesses barely off the
ground already falling to pieces.

That is until she created her own talk to yourself in house radio show, and her Sniffy series in the rehearsal studio area of her website

However, beneath the apparent non-activity of the year when nothing was published, during hours and months of self-healing via free flow journal writing an unusual dossier of incidents, observations, commentary, and clarity of sorts emerged!

Within that dossier themes and patterns seem to take the lead with ideas not facts, but ideas, highly creative ideas at that about leading causes and side-effects possibly hidden or apparent behind ongoing incidents came to prominence.

The acute observation of the difference between how things feel which is not necessarily always the same as fact, and what else might be observed or flagged up during an incident occurring or being perceived as such was another prominent theme which emerged during what was at time moment to moment creation of this dossier initially saved as document 47 prior to being renamed as: **HACK ₒ WEEN**!

Education, educating, and learning during free flow journal sessions is of paramount importance to the self-healing process, and is the intention behind all healing works shared.

Trauma dramas are often some of the most riveting, and captivating experiences you will ever read, watch or experience from any creator. As realizations may spring you out from behind fogged up thinking, bringing out the chilling, and thrilling plot twists to any ongoing experience which may have kept you buried from your own truth and the fullness of your own present day life, your history, and the story about your life you tell yourself which may or may not be in alignment with what is really true.

2014-2024

It has been an intense10 years for the poet who was forced to learn, and without any doubt know the difference between immediate opportunity, leading to financial freedom, and immediate financial opportunity possibly leading you deeper lack of freedom, or further debt. Someone had been hiding behind the wool over someone's eyes. It had been a scenario which left you feeling unfortunate, as though you were being forced to live in someone else's mind game which was actually a health concern with symptoms which presented as a setup where no one can really win, especially, if convinced they are trusting life as normal.

If only there was a neutral or centralized financial system which allowed, you to be paid directly for work you did. Allowing you to work wherever, for whoever as a result all you would have to do is just put into a computerized system your working details, identify yourself, and what type of work you did or most important the financial help you need, and get paid very handsomely for it, or access funds just because you need to cover your cost of living effectively. Such a system could cause less loss, poverty, and financial problems in general for a lot of people already going through a lot of hardship the social impact would be huge, as it inevitable is when writing from a personal perspective in a biographical way, simply because we are all living in change, and momentous moments whether we recognize our lives lived like that or not.

What happened to the World?

What happened to the world?
Seriously, what happened to the world?
What happened to the health, wealth,
and happiness of all groups of people
around the world?
Who really couldn't do the math?
Who let that scam become what it has?
Who thought they could control the
mass by convincing them that less can
still stretch?
Who did that?
Why is life still like that?
Who set up the formula which would
allow anyone's brain to look at that as
accurate?
What happened to the world?
Without any unreasonable doubt people
found a way around that but suppose
within all the success people have made
you never call someone rich again?

Suppose we all stop focusing on the millions, billions, or trillions, and on and on to however many amounts people have made attained or inherited as being rich?

What if we now see it as being the normality it is, and we remain focused on that?

Suppose we just stop focusing on people that are living adequately healthily as normal should be?

Suppose the end of the poverty mindset is to never call anyone rich again?

Suppose the calculation of who is rich and who isn't created what in this book will be called the stretch?

The Stretch

How does 70% stretch to become 500% or to a 1000% without multiplication or addition?
You would need to make the lesser amount equate to the larger amount by maintaining the lesser amount
True or false?
If health depends on it, and ill health can be prevented without it
Is the stretch a scam?

What do you need to do for a human race to have anyone among them believe that would fit and that would do?
What really motivates people to get up and meet their cost of living the way they need to?
Especially, if already ambitious and achieving then knocked off that stool and needs a little help because they were attacked and need a little help?
How does that equate to needing to prove an incapability to move when your income has been removed and no automated payment is automatically given and this is about life, and living?
What happened to the world?
Everyone just got up and ran with it?
People trying to help just couldn't see a lesser amount doesn't stretch it takes a certain quality of food to stop the body from being sick!

What happened to the world?
Or more accurately people in this world?
She got out from underneath us
The gravitation set
Assimilating feelings similar to what
happened back in the days of
plantation living, barely living!
On her work
On her work
What do you do?
Why is that the question that is asked
too soon?
Wanting to be friendly but who are
they really for that to be the question?

The Gravitation Set

Is the term Stalker now inappropriate?
Does the term lecherous make the
problem easier to understand quicker?
Few would understand the mention of a
return to a plantation style of
treatment.
It may offend
That is not what we intend
Within abuse there are several layers to
that kind of treatment
The mention refers to holding a
mindset and opinion over someone not
to be free whilst appearing to live or
even work beside them normally, but
there is no peace

Though streets run quiet, and people
sleep it is how they continue to abuse
you blatantly in front of everybody.
Remotely
Surreptitiously
There again and in the end suppose you
just cannot get up again at least for a
while
Suppose you just can't get up again
genuinely for a while because you still
cannot get yourself ready and don't
want to play a lie?
The burden of something becoming so
impossible the truth cannot be told
about the truth
But inadvertently or directly it is not
about you
Yet it affects you and your innocence
too!

The truth has so many truths
So many ways of saying what true
Every lie has a truth
Every lie probably is the truth in what is
omits, and doesn't say to you
What is selected and what is left for
you?
It just kinder, and more respectful to
make sure you are the one who has said
it
Rather than leaving it to time to reveal
it
The truth is a composite of varying
things which is also calculative
How else to investigations happen?
So, how does it stretch?
The life dependent stretches?
The invention of which affects every
single mindset whether they have had
to live by it or not

That on which life depends hurting the
innocent yet into this modern day
there is an again
The extend
For that which living in life needs
Why shalt they be shamed stalked and
followed to and from their livelihood
until back to that stretch they are
forced to return
There again
Openly flogged at night
Because their lights stop flashing by
daylight!
What happened to their heads?
What was done to their brain?
What caused them trauma?
What damage?
How have their minds been affected?

Was it being forced to live in the stretch for that many years that made just about every situation for them change, or become worse again?

Escapism from hatred and dread?
The escapism of causing the hatred and the dread!
Escaping further and further into a fantasy of leaning in or following others or the one deemed successful?

Like that one person, or those individuals don't need their own peace of mind and space to live without the unwanted attention or unsolicited advice of others which put paid to them living as normal

How much would not have squelched
had there have been no stretch?

If you know it is the currency the
money is how people meet their cost of
living.
People got to work to meet their cost of
living
Which in most cases in today's world is
money that goes into a person's bank
account!

Knowing that is the case, why is the
ability to move and not move the
determining factor as to whether you
can get help or not, especially when
unacceptable circumstances such a non-
apparent flogging applies?

Even the supposed lying man with a bad back
still working
The audacity of a fraud system
Still claiming to have not enough to live off,
and the stretch is not the crime?
When you know what is really needed to live
life
This is about life
How did stringent measure get in where no
limit should appear?
Bullies appear on every street
Stalking campaigns personally, politically,
professionally cost everybody
Bullies appear on every street follow me
I tell you what to eat
How much you will get to live
We'll it all up
We'll break it all down
Fragment to where the most pleasurable will
go
Make that into a profit
In fact after not providing enough we'll take
some back

That will loosen the slack reverse that stretch
with oppressive techniques of enough fear you
won't be awake for years.
Barely make it a law and make dam sure it is
never easy to go to court

With the stretch so cleverly devised how do
rape survivors survive?

If a rape survivor wanted to live ethically
after rape?
How do they do so in a clearly and carefully
carved out "them and us" society?

When there is a very clear message that you
can make much more money if you use or sell
sex?

If you want to be ethical about money and not all interest in the sexuality or the subject of sex is steeped in the experience of being raped. But, if as a result of being raped a survivor doesn't want to live a life where is used as a discipline? The nature of all things to get what you need and want but all around them from investments to funding, to survival is money from people selling sex in every possible conceivable format, then what?

WITH & WITHOUT
SIDE EFFECTS

It is as simple as products to as many people
Or so it would appear
It is as simple as bums on seats
Or so it would appear
It is as simple as focus and prepare
Or so it would appear
It is a simple as the food you eat
Or so it would appear
It is as simple as changing how you feel
Or so it would appear
Which feels better to say?
Which feels better to omit?
There is always something you can do to
change whatever it is you are going through
Unless baffled again!

DEALING WITH TERMS AND CONDITIONS

The term" hack" has various meanings however, in the dossier of sorts the emphasis is really the term when used in conjunction with unauthorized access to a person's personal data, filtering life as an early survivor of rape this meaning seems apt for works.

The term "o" often stands in as a form of punctuation.

The term "ween" again has more than one meaning which seems to relate to not quite having something but having an expectation or intention...or a wish or hope to gain something which maybe the driving force or even motive behind the word to hack gaining unauthorized access to another person's data, the act of needing to gain access, or get, or expect to have.

It is an interesting combination of words as it has been experiences.

But who are the real HACK o WEENS asks characters Executive and Function

HACK O WEEN

Trauma Dramas

Episode 1

"What the bloody hell has been going on...I thought she was all washed up, and gone...where she been working?" Executive

"Well...that's just it.... something's wrong with her.... she..." says Function

"Spit it out!" Executive

"I'm affected...if you don't mind, I'll get it out when I can. It's as the beginning says..."

"What beginning?" Shouts Executive

"...of this book where...the bit where it says about knowing the difference...i mean seeing through to the truth of financial opportunities..." explains Function

"Oh...dear...if that's the way this is going then we are all in trouble."
Executive

"Why?" Function

"Cause, we know we ani't been running it right at all!" Executive

"Why, is that?" Function

"Because there is such a thing as...well...somebody got possessive...I dare to say...."
Executive

"What?" Function

"We had been thinking we could use it to get ahead of the years of mystery surrounding the minimum...!" Executive

"Poet....do you mean medium...what have you done?" Function

"Everything, we could possibly think of" Executive

"What against her?" Function

"Thats not how it first started or came across. I only just...the whole thing...oh...my...God. The whole thing just fell in on me as I realized what you were saying....and took for granted where she should be knowing she doesn't have anyting in terms of cost of living finance, or ready cash...it didn't occur to me the pressure that would be on her...I'm so...." Executive

"What.... you are so, what exactly?" Function asks with great annoyance

"I'll cooperate. None of us ever really saw it like that until today. The partitioning of someone without keeping them locked up in a house. Yet, a form of partitioning arose in public, somehow, we managed it." Executive

"You mean, every time she went out? Everywhere she went. You were all out there after her? Just like she said and sang in her ah way yah stalking me fah single...or whatever it is called...umm...it

changed didn't it she called it
Deliberate Drama…didn't she…"
says Function

"This isn't just about stalking…this is
also about her changing the way
she has dealt with her past."
Executive

"Oh…yes…well, given her past
includes rape why would she or
anyone else with that kind of past
be able to say they have been
stalked? Hmmm…think about it…"
Function

"Didn't she say in the dossier, a
winning card for everybody?"
Executive

"Yeah…well if she did what does
that really mean for anyone,
without everyone understanding

about getting behind the why?
With what? popular amongst
whom with what? Do what you are
doing, but for who with what?
There is no get out clause with this
Ai." Function

"There is no get out clause with any
Ai period which is relative to life. it is
all very plain to see as the
evidence is so strong above
everybody, with anything."
Executive

"Budgets surely differ. They must be
different. Possibly a very big
difference.... there is a difference
between building Authentic
Intelligence as opposed to building
Artificial intelligence, but each
state says exactly what each state
is, with the debate remaining as to
the different side effects each

might have on the world around us be that by choice or by force...but without all that weighing in for some reason today just felt like the longest journey of someone having finished a domestic abusive relationship, moved on with their life, only to find the abusers had taken over just about everything in their life specifically the financial area of their life leaving them without, and feeling trapped and unfree, with no idea where to go to never be affected again."
Function
"Come on, it's not that bad"
Executive

"What? are you too scared to look at it for what it is the accurate way round?" Function

"I can't do this" Executive

"Why not what have you been and done? What's got into you? you said you would cooperate?" Function still shouting

"Hang on a minute, I think she's found it..." Executive

"Found, what?" Function

"Well, she claimed she started that dossier in late summer 2023...but it looks like she has just found and opened the original copy before she renamed it Hack o Ween...and it became about 250 pages long" Executive

"Well...go on what's in it...what's she said? What's the exact time and date?" Function

"Hold on...I'll have a look..."
Executive

"02/09/2023/06:51 content creation date" Executive

"Yeah...that is still late summer...how does it start off?" Function

"I'm not going to waste any time reading it out...I'll just cut copy and paste it to below" Executive

HoW: The most dangerous people are the ones who are under everything, but do not feel at liberty to say anything? or who are not at liberty to say anything? Like the truth they really know

True or False?

HoW: Until you understand the brokenness that comes from being stalked will you understand the effect upon someone who is being stalked, and the detriment upon one's life if dismissed due to mentioning you are indeed continually targeted!

True or False?

HoW: Back in the day what were people inventing, operating, managing, and using as authority over people, and necessary resources for life to be what it is?
Oppositional Defiance?
Spite?
Sleight?
Mean Fistedness?
Lack of foresight or insight?

What type of damage to the brain could cause any of these things in all of us?

"I don't know" Executive
"Is that it...what else has she written as Hack o Ween the HoW" Function
"I don't know..." Executive
"The truth is you don't know because your mind is more than likely closed off after following who led you behind wool over eyes...
...go down it let's see what else she has written..." Function
HoW: For it to be possible for rapist and very violent people to even meet others not like them, or date persons which do not have matching behaviours. Is the system of voting "presented" as politics responsible for what could possibly be amongst the biggest health

scams ever blatantly made, allowed, and continued? Which may beggar the question what exactly is being voted for, if not the continuation of that which may lead to murder?

"You What...that's a bit farfetched and out of line...people stepped into stop extreme behaviours.... really.... it's the fact...?" a shocked Function asks

"Yeah...that's trauma...I know it's the fact it goes from something seemingly unconnected and simple to murder.... well, you said go down it and see what emerged, and this is it, and there is more...keep looking...the brain keeps traumatizing things together or so it would appear" Executive

Considering sugar kills and is still widely available
"Hmm…. mmm…this isn't good…or is it…this is totally weirded out… this is uncomfortable" exclaims Function
"…and you were on about what had I done….to think of it" Executive
Tobacco and vaping kills, and again is still widely available

"What…she is not messing with us now…she has got some nerve, and she is still writing…this is the beginning of the dossier, and this is what is coming up for her after her last series Fanaticism…" Executive

"Oh yeah…I had almost forgotten about that series…that is why this is coming up next, then" Function

HoW: What is so called politics can at times appear as nothing more than the freedom of behaviours which may include narcissistic and sadistic narcissistic supply and all the continuums related to incestuous rape, and high scale deviant sexual behaviours. Most possibly cleverly disguised practices which have led to the disorientation of mass brain function as a result controlling the mindset on mass right down to the money.

"It's weird but is this what politics looks like to someone who never thought they would ever get to report the crimes brought against them from a baby to a child?"
Executive

UNDIVINE SERVICE @

Elem' o Clock

Let Us Prey

Our Traumas

Which are not in heaven
Hallowed was not thy name
Thy will has not yet been done
Thy kingdom did not come on earth,
but thy healing will feel more like a
heaven
Though hath not forgiven us this day
But continues to trespass against
Thine was not the kingdom
nor the power or the glory
However, there shall be no more abuse
from thy rouse
As that reign of terror which had
haunted us forever will be overcome

HACK o WEEN
Episode 2

Trauma along the M25 from Junctions 5 & 6
to Junction 9, A243 toward A3 London bound

08/10/23/04:59
A faint high telephone type female voice
says, "you need to make "...." of how
they did this to me"
A louder resounding voice with a thin
gauntish face says I used a one inch?

_____

Saw clairvoyance of a thin fighting
person angry character, literally
punching back toward living energy.

For what we are about to eat the Lord
make us truly ungrateful for if the
ungrateful did not speak they and
gratitude could not meet?

09/10/2023/0200-0300 M25 JUNCT 5-6

"STOP!" shouts Function "Stop…for goodness' sake…and allow me…I said I would cooperate…these are very sensitive works because it is coming from a document of origin. STOP!" Executive

"You better come up with the best narrative or explanation you have got. I think, I know what this is but if not delivered in the best conceivable way it could…upset the wrong side of things, and let me please say…I am truly grateful, for the grateful and ungrateful alike…" Function

"Ok...so...look...it all first seems to have begun appearing on Fridays only...the activity as far as she was forced to observe seemed to be ramped up on a Friday, mostly evening to night because that was her preferred shift pattern..."
Executive

"But...we are talking here or referring to the patterns of behaviours she herself has only been able to describe as those associated with, or similar to stalking activities, right?" asks Function

"Something like that..." Executive

"Something...like...that...what the hell have your lot been thinking like?" Function asks in utter frustration

"Let me...finish. Just let me finish...I know what this sounds like...but let me get this out...because of the leaning toward spiritualism in all its possible forms of communication appearing to be present...right, so this had gone on since...well...to a greater or lesser degree most noticeable from since 2018..." Executive

"More noticeable..." notes Function

"Well...because it began as a non-apparent mess in 2014..." Executive

"Incidents..." Function attempts to direct Executive

"Stay with me on this one…mess…almost impossible to detect outside of those who created it or had it planned right down to the t…" Executive

"Is that a tee?" Function asks

"Yes…anyway do let me continue. It would appear the whole thing was devised in such a way only the Poetical author would be seen to be at fault despite a growing number of participants that would appear to appear as an entourage." Executive
"So, how is that suspicious?" Function
"What…someone who is supposedly not being stalked by anybody, doing not much more than activities associated with her funding her cost of living…even in

creativity wouldn't accrue such an interest without a stalker somewhere amongst the activity being of interest, and interested." Executive

"Oh...seen got it...go on because we both said stop at the same time...it was HoW going in the direction of spiritualism, again so soon into the beginning of the document...but the plot twist is interesting to me." Function

"The plot twist is quite frankly dangerous. Back in the day for some folks as they get older life becomes more relaxing, not more chaotic hectic, or violent...not only that when incidents are happening at work where employment law is very clearly written there is more to it than just a concern." Executive

"The plot twist is not so much of a twist. The mention of twist just refers to a moment of change of direction regarding realization occurs which in this case was one simple word or more of a phrase, and that happened when for some reason a collection of past relationships began to haunt her. She woke up to an epiphany, and experienced a very spiritual moment as the relationship was described as being with someone who deliberately baffled.... did you hear that...a high American sounding spirit said: Thank you"
Function

"Our work within spirit I still think is often misunderstood, a gravity vaster than we could imagine. A voice during editing also repeated did you hear that! Actually, I think the whole "entourage" of ongoing rounds of cars experienced as abuse in the workplace was probably the baffler trying to compete against spiritualism whilst suffering from their own fear whilst being able to baffle not just one person, but many. Very blatantly?" Executive

"You only get like that when you have been able to pull strings off unnoticed, or because you were noticed but were prepared and able enough to baffle all the way through. See, it's one thing to criticize people like politicians and lawmakers for getting it wrong. But why were they put there in the first place? I'll tell you why, more than likely because of a baffler-a deliberate cause maker...what else you got from what she's written?" Function

"It's a difficult document for me to negotiate, if I'm honest." Executive

"The real juice...get to that...let's think about what that is, and by that, I mean if we are going to dwell anywhere then it is in the root causes!" Function

"Well, if anything explains it is where we said STOP at." Executive

HoW: Here: 09/10/2023/0200-0300 M25 JUNCT 5-6

"What's been going on at that location?" Function

"Well, in brief..." Executive

"Wait...she had to have moved on again...for there to be ongoing problems...I bet..." Function

"She was planning to publish works as normal per year. However, due to a change in the way she has been dealing with abuse and getting back on her feet after illness and injury at work, she finds herself unable to focus, and the urgency to keep something in print finally flexes and trundles off to the back burner. For the first time in a long time, she felt opposed to answering the call to write...and yes, she did move on again...without even thinking about it or trying to find evidence or reason for things which had long eluded her. As unbelievable as it sounds, she found for some reason every time she travelled in the area of the United Kingdom Motorway network area of the M25 junction 5 & 6 she felt like she was straining to stay awake. This was whether she had a good night's brain resetting sleep or not. Even if she had just had a power nap whilst on a bay unloading or not. That area of the motorway would affect her brain functioning. She describes feelings such as her hair being dragged back. Nobody was in the vehicle at the time who could touch her. However, she also described struggling with people as they drove past her, literally feeling pulled downwards, and feeling knocked out of her senses...returning to base aka transport office physically, let alone physiologically shaken, and disturbed by events she just couldn't understand let alone control." Executive

"Yeah...I remember this coming up...you are right...this began from 2014 when she again was returning to work after her work and living conditions were affected causing, illness, and injury this had affected her life before...but...actually out on road this came up more than once..." Function remembers

"Well, look, let's put this together because there is obviously something very serious going on here, and someone possibly has a very dangerous intention toward her by now. There is an area of stalking behaviours known as grudge stalking given what has gone on from about 2006, there may be some kind of connection.

Worst case scenario this goes back to childhood." Executive

"Well, what I have got is this...I vaguely remember that in 2014, that she found it very odd that she found it very difficult to remain consciously awake despite sleeping through rest periods, or periods of availability at work for up to 2 to 3 hours, after only driving for the most part 2.5 to 3.5 if that...worst case scenario routes back then would be a drive of the obligatory 4.5 hours. Even though rest periods of only 9 hours with 2 hour commute either side could give cause for concern. There was enough time to catch at the very least a power naps, which on many occasions had been enough to suffice the longest of working days without incident." Function

"Hmm...so what went wrong this time with this little "baffle them under plan" do you think?"
Executive

"Well, clearly the timer went off"
Function

"Excuse me, the timer?" Executive

"Well, the orientation then...satnav must have been reprogrammed to become obvious" Function

"What are you talking about?"
Executive

"Something must have gone very wrong...I just remember what she said. What we can't work out is how the baffle is the baffle, and why or who has brought the baffle to come about to keep us baffled out?" Function

"So, what is the baffle?" Executive

"Right, I worked it out as the baffle being that she is forced to feel like she is falling asleep, against her will, and the logic that she has had enough sleep to function properly." Function

"Ok...I would have thought the baffle was keeping us all focused on her?" Executive

"Nah...the next bit is...she is only being made to feel like she is losing concentration, and consciousness only in certain areas...there..." Function

"I have noted those years and areas as follows: from since 2014 M40 toward junction 3 & 4 down toward Junction 1 M25 where it splits to Dartford, and Heathrow areas." Executive

"The areas where she has been affected change because she kept up work changes, which is possibly how she can prove this is stalking because the areas of occurrences kept changing" Function

"Well, from 2014, the next "batch" incidents of ongoing attacks of unconsciousness, spiritualist medium activities? Brain deactivation began occurring..." Executive

"I remember her saying it now…began occurring after she come off the M25 junction toward the M20 as she would follow to the right and go along the M20 toward where the motorways would merge as she would be headed toward about junction 5 to 6 of the M20 where the lanes would feed off toward Aylesford, and Maidstone areas. I remember her saying she found it very difficult to go down the darkest area of the motorway, which would possibly be around the 3rd or 4th junction area, but there has been modification to that area of road therefore may not be deemed as a junction. However, she would get ever so annoyed because drivers with international vehicle registration plates coming along the opposite carriage way would almost always flash stun her with their headlights but no other drivers. This would occur soon after she drove past the exit continuing along the M20." Function

"That is two locations down...isn't it..." Executive

"Wait...no please...wait...didn't she document, and depict in art an incident some years ago on East Finchley High Road...a bit up from the post office near a supermarket, but on the opposite side of the road...where this woman kind of brunette to strawberry blonde, with a brow length fringe, slim in a black floral smart but casual dress, possible with shoulder length handbag...she was leaning backwards in the street in the strangest of poses?" Function

"Yes, but as far as I am aware she hasn't lived in that area officially since October 2013, and she had only moved in that area in June 2009...if I find..." Executive

"Listen, you think about it suppose this is like gospel call and response? But instead, this is display then do?" Function

"If you are saying what I think you are saying, that means what is happening now had been preplanned all those years in advance? How the devil was she supposed to know or be forewarned of that showing up when it did, suppose....im just thinking of who that individual might be? Who were her connections? For whom could they have been working? If they were targeting her, when did it begin, and why would they plan to attack her at work?" Executive

"Look at you trying to play the innocent party after all those years of getting ahead...so what have we got so far on this because it's wearing me out" Function

"Right, 2014 it begins in the area of M40, as you said from about Junction 3 & 4 onwards toward M25 at junction 1 M40 becomes A40 and goes through toward Greenford areas, toward Hanger Lane, toward Marylebone, Euston, Kings cross running parallel to the heart of the West End of London, however Lavinia's journeys were taking her toward A12 area of the M25 during those years. Then, from 2018, she changes work, and the abuse is ramped up, again. Now she is frequently traveling along the M25 to take-up the M20. This up until and possibly a little after Covid-19, where again she changes but returns to where she had worked before, and finds attacks go off the chart. During that time, she starts to observe difficulties with the same style whether you call it brain deactivations, she feels sleep occurring as she turns off the motorway or main roads toward base..." Executive is interrupted

"As she leaves the entourage of drive by stalkers you mean?"

"Possibly, prospective employers however, by now she has released music but has basically little to no social media attention for her works so the reason for such attention doesn't make sense to her. As her work moves further afield the targeting is constant in a form of what seems like large entourages not of her own making, but from about 2018 it definitely seems yet again to be work based. Areas of the M74 impacted her but she also observed that in conjunction to seeing particular hauliers vehicles she feels a direct impact because she would automatically lose consciousness, and again physically feel forced to sleep, or be straining to be stop the impact on her. But certainly left feeling battered by non-apparent assault whilst working. From about

2020 to about 2022 may have been the most varied occurrences of the same incident of being forced to sleep, or all of sudden getting to the same area of motorway and feeling knocked out or eyes forced shut this was ongoing possibly since before 2020 whenever she got to about the Junction 16 area of the M6 where she describes a widening of the motorway area, and a flattening of the land where what looks abandoned trailers are kept with mannequins with Mother and baby can be seen in the fields beside the motorway. By June of 2022, her ability to work suddenly came to a halt, there were no incidents again until from about March 2023 because she hadn't been back at work," Executive

"I mean, I am absolutely stunned. I really am that things could have gone wrong for this long. Now I have looked at it all as a list of incidents. It's a horrible thing to think you can't trust life without things like this happening" Function

"But you can trust life, these types of incidents are not the norm, a list can only be created because something initially was ignored, misunderstood, not paid attention to, and all these things could happen without any intention of sleight or intention of harm, my concern is why it is been done?" Executive

"Maybe, it is because she was too trusting, or trusting in the right way, in the way we are supposed to trust life. But I must admit it feels grudge like, the only other thing that comes up for me within it is possibly someone's grudge toward being left with children as farfetched as that might sound" Function

"Because she used to be a registered childminder, didn't she. But she has never been quiet or understated about the level of rape and violence she herself went through as a child. The very fact you could know that and still not be able to stop yourself from attacking someone, or anyone with that type of experience, the failure and the folly is not due to how those type of survivors need to survive, especially if you are also attacking them because you are having the same or similar experience as bizarre as that may sound. I think there is some other

need driving such actions."
Executive
"Nobody is less deserving of help than another." Function
"I agree, I think we can now better understand how a winning card for everybody can work, and why there is an almost silent terror, and frustration with a financial system which can be so easily exploited by those suffering from the need to administer cruelty, and spite in an attempt to control and abuse others. It is easy to see, that if a system could be devised the power to attack would be lessened...hopefully" Executive

"That has come up directly from experiences of not being paid directly after completing works, being accused of walking out of the job which she had finished, and that having become a pattern of threat thankfully not everywhere...but to be honest in the UK, she, and a ton of other companies have been hit hard by scammers, business gangs, using god knows what to lure people out of funds, making promises to what was previously thought of inaccessible? During this time she also described problems with a look-a-like industry which she was also been targeted by, which has left her accused." Function

"Problem solving is also an industry which you would think could tackle and solve such issues, yet such services are not always as obvious to contact or interact with. I think we are about done here."
Executive

Natural Flowism
A
Freedom of Being!

Created in and inspired
by
life in the UK

Message from Author

I am so Thankfully, Grateful, and Blessed by the Spirit of God, as I Repent, and Surrender to the Forgiveness, Power, and Purpose Life is.

A big thank you to my loving daughter, my inspiration who has been through and put up with so much!

Blessings, and Greetings to all who are able to accept.

Thank You to all who have managed to read, and understand my books, they are not all easy to understand, as some books I was only just about able to edit due the intensity of trauma affecting my brain during the time of writing.

76

Thank You to Amazon for making Self-Publishing Possible

Thank You to all in the World of Transport & Logistics for doing their very best to keep businesses and services running smoothly despite all challenges faced

Thank You to Amen Clinics and BrainMD for helping the world become a healthier, happier, and more knowledgeable place to be by making learning about our brain so easy, and so accessible!

Brain Health mentioned
Courtesy of Amen Clinics
www.amenclinics.com

𝕭lack 𝕯ynasties?

JOURNEY FROM THE EQUATOR TO COLOUR AS BEHAVIOUR

∧

You'll be lucky in this life if what you want for yourself is also what others want for you.
Often times what others want for you is not what you want for yourself.
Others may view what you do as having a status which does not belong to you.

∧

Though your status may change others may not view that as the same as you do.
Because others say your status has changed doesn't mean it has changed!

∧

Lessons of worthiness in this life are not about letting a person know how much you may value them...it is to understand if they even know or understand the term value in relation to themselves. If this perspective could be understood expectation would never leave so many feeling heartbroken abandoned and wary!

#laviniadeayr

BRAIN
TRAUMA
DAMAGE
MIND
AFFECTED

A
REMINDER
TO
SELF
A
WINNING
CARD
FOR
EVERYBODY
MEANING
TO
RESPECT
EVERYBODY
CAN
WIN
NO
MATTER
WHAT
THEY
HAVE
BEEN
PUT

THROUGH
MAINTAINING
RESPECT
FROM
THE
STRETCH
TO
A
WINNING
CARD
FOR
EVERYBODY
NO
UNWANTED
ATTENTION
NO
ACCUSATION
JUST
LEARNING
THE
BALANCE
AND

RESPECT
NEEDED
FOR
EACH
AND
EVERYONE!
MUCH
LOVE
MUCH
APPRECIATED
ABUNDANT
THANKS
AND
ENDLESS
AMOUNTS
OF
GRATITUDE
LIFE
IN
A
LIFE
WITHOUT

LIMITS
BUT
WHAT
MADE
THEM
THINK
LIKE
THAT
WHAT
MADE
THEM
CREATE
THE
STRETCH
WAS
IT
BRAIN
TRAUMA
DAMAGE
MIND
AFFECTED
=

NATURAL

FLOWISM

A

FREEDOM

OF

BEING!

www.naturalflowism.com